Reset Your Relationship with Food: How to Ditch Your Disordered Eating

by Stephanie Eissinger, MA, LCPC, CPC

This is a 1st Edition.

Reset Your Relationship with Food: How to Ditch Your Disordered Eating

A Sagebrush Coaching & Counseling Services, PPL Book

PUBLISHING HISTORY

Sagebrush Coaching & Counseling paperback March 2017

For Information address: www.sagebrushcoaching.com

ISBN-13: 978-1540852380

ISBN-10: 1540852385

Dedication

This book is dedicated to all the women I have been blessed to know in both my personal and professional life. Being female is challenging with all the contradictory and confusing messages about femininity and success we receive from our culture, the media, our family, and our friends. My goal is to make that challenge less daunting. It's to empower women to take back their lives, embrace their own unique brand of beauty, and to honor their bodies by teaching them a different mindset.

A mindset that frees them from the grip of disordered eating patterns, self loathing, and ultimately self-destruction. A mindset that frees their voices and gives them the power to love their bodies "as is," seize the opportunities that life presents, overcome obstacles, and define beauty and success however they choose!

TABLE OF CONTENTS

Acknowledgments

I would like to express my gratitude to all the professionals I learned from – there are too many to list – and the clients I've had the honor to work with who have taught me a great deal, probably more than I could ever have taught them.

And I want to acknowledge all the thick skinned and insensitive people who came and went in my life. I now see you for what you truly were – a gift. You forced me to learn the skills to make my voice heard, to get my needs met, to stand up for myself, and to speak the truth even when that truth was unpopular.

I will be forever grateful to you all!

Introduction

The hallmark of disordered eating is a pattern of destructive eating behavior that results in compulsive overeating, restrictive eating that includes excessive restriction of the types of food eaten (as with the severe adherence to a "clean eating" diet), binging with or without purging, using food to numb feelings (known as "emotional eating") and/or yo-yo dieting. These negative eating patterns are often coupled with a distorted body image and poor self esteem and self confidence. One of the keys that will unlock the chains that bind us so tightly to unhealthy eating behavior is to reset our relationship with food. We must come to a new understanding of what food really means to us – it's not necessarily the same for everyone.

For example, for me, food represented control. When I was a young adolescent, so many areas of my life felt out of my control...but, I *could* control what I ate, when I ate, and how much I ate. I could control when I exercised and to what degree. And, I could control my feelings by constricting them to the point that I felt almost nothing at all. Growing up I learned that feeling too much, and worse yet, allowing others to know the depth of my feelings was unacceptable – a flaw to be ridiculed and dismissed.

This book is an expression of my passion to empower others who are emotionally sensitive to learn the skills necessary to survive in a culture that rewards and praises self control, stoicism, and the ability to pull oneself up by their bootstraps. I want every woman out there to know that even though she may feel "too" much, see "too" much, and intuitively know "too" much, there is NOTHING wrong with her. Our society would be better served if more people were as emotionally sensitive and highly intuitive as she.

I hope this book will be instrumental in a powerful transformation in these women's lives – a transformation that honors their gifts of compassion, unique inner beauty, and strength. One that enables them to use that very compassion to build a more loving and accepting relationship with themselves, not just others; a respectful and loving alliance with their bodies; and a healthier, less conflicted relationship with food.

I want everyone who struggles with food and weight issues to discover how to transform their lives, find their passion and purpose, and ditch their disordered eating once and for all. It's a gift I would bestow on every woman, child, and man if it were in my humble power to do so. I can only hope that this book is read and absorbed by some, who then share it with others, and that the ripple effect will spread in an ever widening circle of compassion, love, and wisdom....

Chapter One:

EXPLORING YOUR RELATIONSHIP WITH FOOD

"Food is fabulous, and having a good relationship with it will make you healthy and happy."

Denise Austin

Several elements interact to influence your relationship with food, elements that determine if it's a healthy relationship or if it's unhealthy and part of a destructive cycle. These elements include: historical factors, current attitude/mindset towards food, food "story," and food aptitude. Exploring each of these factors in depth will help you to better assess your current relationship with food and its origins.

This chapter is designed to help you do a "deep dive" into your relationship with food and what beliefs, attitudes or mindset, and skill deficiencies may need to be addressed in order to ditch your disordered eating pattern for good.

HISTORICAL FACTORS: To begin exploring your relationship with food, go back to your childhood. Sifting through your food related memories and the emotions that have become tied to food through your experiences can be instrumental in figuring out food related patterns that are concerning to you.

Your first experiences with food and how food was viewed in your home growing up sets the foundation for how you think about food later in life. Unless you become aware of how this relationship was formed and make a conscious effort to change it, it will continue operating in the background and influencing the role that food takes in your life. Writing down your responses to the following questions will provide you with a reference you can come back to whenever you're struggling with eating when you're *not* physically hungry or *not* eating when you are.

1. **What messages did I receive about food, diets, and meals when I was growing up?**

- Were certain foods labelled "good" or "bad?"

- Was breakfast the "most important meal of the day" or was it viewed as something to be skipped due to hurried morning schedules?

- What was your mother's relationship with food? Did she diet a lot? Did she worry about her weight?

- What was your father's relationship with food? Was it used for fuel or refuge? Was it healthy or unhealthy?

- How about the relationship with food that other significant family members exhibited? (grandparents, aunts, uncles, siblings, cousins, etc.)

2. **What was my family's general attitude toward healthy and unhealthy food?**

- Were rich, heavy foods the usual fare at meal times with lots of junk food in the pantry for snacking?

- Were there only "healthy" foods available that were unappetizing but the latest fad?

- Were a majority of the meals served nutritious, but other foods available in moderation?

3. **What associations have I maintained in relation to certain foods?**

- Was food used for comfort? (i.e. Mom made me macaroni & cheese whenever I had a bad day at school.)

- Was food used as a reward? (i.e. Dad would take me out for ice cream whenever I got an "A" on one of my papers.)

- Was food used for celebrating? (i.e. Huge meals were served as a major part of every celebration and everyone was expected to overeat until they were miserable.)

- Was food restriction used as a punishment? (i.e. Childish misbehavior was punished by being sent to bed without supper.)

- Was mealtime a battleground? (i.e. My brother wasn't allowed to leave the table until he ate everything on his plate. Being the "perfect" child, I ate everything even if I was full to please my parents.)

- If I answered yes to any of the above questions, do I continue to use food in this way? Write down specific examples.

Answering the above questions, and any others that come up during your exploration, will help clarify historical food messages that may be influencing your current relationship with food. You may be explicitly following these messages or you may be "rebelling" against them without even realizing it.

CURRENT ATTITUDE TOWARDS FOOD: The second element that influences your relationship with food is your current attitude toward it. This attitude stems from the internal dialogue you have related to nourishing your body with calories and specific foods. Paying attention to the language you use in relation to food and how you talk to yourself about food and eating will provide you with insights that will help you make any "attitude adjustments" required for resetting your relationship with food, yourself, and your body.

1. **How do I view food?**

- Do I see it as a source of nutritional value to meet my body's needs?

- Are food and calories viewed as the "enemy?"

- Is food seen as a vehicle for immediate comfort?

2. **What is the strongest emotion that I feel when I think about eating? (guilt, shame, pleasure, etc.)**

An important piece of understanding your relationship with food is becoming aware of what you're saying to yourself about food and how you feel when you're faced with mealtimes and food decisions. This awareness will enhance your ability to decipher what food may be symbolically representing in your life so that you can deal with the underlying problem directly.

Does your current attitude reflect historical messages? If so, what are those messages?

_____

_____

_____

_____

_____

_____

_____

YOUR FOOD "STORY": Your food story is the justification you use to support your current relationship with food. It's what you tell yourself that supports your eating patterns, food related habits, and any food rules or rituals that you abide by.

My Food Story: While I was actively engaging in anorexic behaviors as an adolescent, the "story" I told myself was that I needed to be perfect so my father would finally be proud of me and so the kids at school wouldn't notice that my family wasn't close and we didn't have a lot of money. The only things I felt I had control over were what and how much I ate, how much effort I put into my behaviors, and how much I exercised in my bedroom late at night when no one was around to interrupt me.

Comments from relatives and admiring questions about how I lost so much weight from "popular" girls reinforced my story. Sadly, my efforts went unnoticed by my father until he became worried that I'd be too weak to do barn chores or ride colts and gather cows all day. Perversely, this too reinforced my disordered eating...even though it was negative, I finally had his attention.

SUMMARIZE YOUR FOOD STORY:

_____
_____
_____
_____
_____
_____

FOOD APTITUDE: Your food aptitude refers to the skills and knowledge you already possess regarding how to nourish your body and eat for optimal health.

1. **What skills and knowledge do I possess related to food, nutrition, and what my body needs to function at an optimal level?**

- Do I know the nutritional value of foods?

- Do I know what calorie intake I need for weight loss, gain, or maintenance?

- Do I have the culinary skills to make healthy foods taste delicious to me?

- Do I know how to provide the appropriate nourishment my body needs according to my activity level? (i.e. energy replacement necessary to fuel my body through tough workouts)

2. **What skills and knowledge am I lacking?**

- Do I need to visit with a nutritionist to develop a plan for my healthy eating goals?

- Do I need to take cooking classes or learn how to use spices to make healthy food taste better?

- Do I need to learn how to convert old "comfort foods" into healthier versions?

Summarize Your Food Aptitude:

_____

_____

_____

_____

_____

Acknowledging deficits in your knowledge and skillset related to eating "healthy" can help you to determine what you need to learn and if you need to enlist the aid of a nutritionist to get you started on the right track.

All of these elements interact with your beliefs about yourself, your body image, your mindset, and the status of your essential life skills. Together they inform and reinforce your current relationship with food, making it impossible for you to sustain long term recovery from disordered eating patterns.

Chapter Two:

Factors That Affect Your Relationship With Food

"Being fully present and aware are the foundation to building a healthy relationship with food."

Jennifer Bolus, RD

There are five main factors that affect your relationship with food: (1) beliefs you hold about yourself & food, (2) your body image, (3) your coping skills/strategies, and (4) your mindset. Breaking free from disordered eating and resetting your relationship with food becomes much simpler once you have an understanding of how these factors influence you.

BELIEFS ABOUT YOURSELF

What you think and believe about yourself and how you consistently talk to and about yourself determines how you feel about yourself. If you perceive yourself as a hopeless overweight loser that doesn't deserve to be happy, you will behave as if it's true. In the same token, if you believe that you're a strong, talented, and attractive winner who deserves to succeed, you'll engage in behaviour that supports that belief.

Answer the following questions honestly and without judging yourself. This exercise is meant to be one of self-discovery, not self-ridicule.

- What do you believe about yourself? *(i.e. "I'm unlovable." "I must be perfect to be loved." "I'm beautiful inside & out." "I'm weak." "I'm resilient." I'm not good enough." "I don't deserve to be happy." "There is something wrong with me.")*_____

   _____

   _____

   _____

- What kinds of things do you say to yourself? *(i.e. "If I put my mind to it, I can do anything." "I'm so fat no one could ever love me." "I'm a loser, everyone thinks so." "Nothing I do is ever good enough." "I'm strong & healthy." "I can do anything I decide to do." "My thunder thighs are disgusting.")*_____

   _____

   _____

   _____

- What labels have you given yourself? *(i.e. "loser," "athlete," "fatty," "weak," "courageous," "resilient")*

   _____

   _____

   _____

   _____

The core beliefs that you have about yourself, the way in which you talk to yourself, and the labels that you give yourself all have a profound effect on how you treat yourself and your body. *If the overall message you're giving yourself is that you're unlovable the way you are, you're not going to value yourself enough to develop and maintain a healthy relationship with food.*

YOUR BELIEF ABOUT FOOD

Here is where you *really* need to pay attention. The following concept is a pivotal shift in what most people who struggle with disordered eating and weight related issues believe about food.

You need to change your belief that

food itself is the *problem*.

Food is *not* the problem. The real problem is what food represents to you – what *function* it serves in your life. The PROBLEM is whatever you're REALLY HUNGRY for and it may be something that you're not even aware of because it's buried in your unconscious mind. The driving force behind disordered eating is the attempt to use food to satisfy a non-physical hunger.

The thing is, most of these underlying hungers stem from

complicated issues that are scary to confront and require a complex set of skills to resolve. If you convince yourself that the problem is that you're a weak willed loser who's obsessed with food, all of these other life problems fade into the background.

Even though thinking about yourself and food in such a negative way is extremely painful, it's still a problem you can easily understand and you have a whole range of options to try to "solve" the problem. Just turn on your television or fire up your computer or smart phone and do a quick search, there is a multitude of choices to try – fad diets and weight loss supplements, pro-anorexia blogs, extreme clean eating programs, etc. And, to make it worse, you will be bombarded with pictures of "ideal bodies" and given the unmistakable message that this unrealistic photo shopped image is how you're "supposed" to look.

The same goes with thinking your weight or your body is the problem. Your weight is *not* the problem. Your body is *not* the problem. These too are distracting elements and food is the most predictable weapon to use if you're at war with your weight or your body. When you become laser focused on any or all of these issues, it's easier to ignore the underlying problems that are harder to decipher. It's much simpler to start yet another fitness program that's in vogue or buy the newest piece of fitness equipment.

Food, body image, and weight are all problems with obvious, yet ultimately self-defeating and/or self-destructive solutions if your non-physical hunger isn't dealt with directly. No amount of food, exercise, or dieting can satisfy or resolve a hunger that is created by a need that remains unfulfilled.

With disordered eating, food serves as the distracting element. If food, weight and your body is your focus, the real issues that are causing your distress never get solved and food continues to be your focus – the foods you want to eat, the foods you don't want to eat, calorie counting, the number on a scale, the fat on your body...it never ends!

Your real issues have to do with emotions, intuitions, and instincts. This doesn't mean that there's something wrong with you. It means you're an emotionally sensitive and perceptive individual who happens to live in an emotionally insensitive world. The good news is that the skills you need to survive and even thrive in such a culture can be learned, practiced, and polished to the point that you're capable of leading the life you want without disordered eating and a distorted body image holding you hostage.

Since you can't change who you are or the circumstances and environment you grew up in, you need to develop a specific skillset in order to function in a world that doesn't honor your unique ability to tune into the emotional realities around you, to perceive subtle nuances, and to feel your and other's pain more intensely. These abilities, when coupled with the right empowerment skills, can make you a powerful ally and advocate for yourself and for others.

YOUR BODY IMAGE

Your body image is NOT what you picture in the mirror. It's the mental representation of how you think and feel about your body that distorts what you see when you gaze at your reflection. It's the lens that you view your body through – and it can be negatively or positively skewed. The following questions will help you assess the status of your body image.

- How do you "feel" *about* your body?

  _____
  _____
  _____
  _____

- How do you "feel" *in* your body?

  _____
  _____
  _____
  _____

- What do you *believe* about your body?

  _____
  _____
  _____
  _____

- What is your "*mental representation*" of what your body looks like?

  _____

  _____

  _____

  _____

If your current body image is distorted and/or negative, you're thoughts and eating behaviors will reflect this. Developing a disordered eating pattern is a common response to having a negative body image. *Learning to "see" your body realistically and accepting it "as is" is a key component to building and maintaining a healthy relationship with food – one in which food is looked at as nourishing energy for the body you love.*

(For more specific body image help, read *How To "Rock" Your Body Image: Improve Body Image & Self Confidence.)

YOUR COPING SKILLS/STRATEGIES

There are certain life skills that are essential for you to develop and practice in order to break the cycle of disordered eating; empower yourself to make healthy changes and take advantage of opportunities; and give yourself the ability to tackle all of life's challenges, regardless of whether they're positive or negative ones.

Continue writing down your responses to the questions...the more specific information you accumulate and bring into your awareness, the easier it will be to determine what skills you need and/or want to develop.

After each skill or strategy you list, make a note of whether it's positive or negative, and how often you actually utilize that particular skill. Remember, be curious and non-judgmental - you're gathering data, not points of criticism.

- What coping skills/strategies do you have for dealing with stress?

_____

_____

_____

_____

_____

_____

- What coping skills/strategies do you have for dealing with strong emotions? (positive & negative)

_____

_____

_____

_____

_____

_____

- What coping skills/strategies do you have for dealing with boredom or "down time?"

_____

_____

_____

_____

_____ -

_____

- What coping skills/strategies do you have for dealing with challenges?

_____

_____

_____

_____

_____ -

_____

The more positive coping strategies or "tools" you have in your life skills toolbox and the more often you practice them, the less likely you will be to turn to negative coping methods, like using food to comfort you when you're feeling distressed or as a distraction from more complex problems. Although food is effective in providing quick relief from emotional distress, that feeling of relief is fleeting and often leads to increased distress in the long run, reinforcing a negative cycle.

The use of food to self-medicate or as a distraction instead of dealing with the complicated and less obvious issues that may be buried below your awareness is the single most powerful factor preventing you from a full and complete break-up with your disordered eating pattern – whether it's overeating, restricting, binging, yo-yo dieting, etc.

YOUR MINDSET

Your mindset includes the way that you view your environment, your perspective, and your locus of control. The following questions will help you to clarify your current mindset and determine whether or not it could benefit from an "adjustment."

- Do you see your environment as friendly or hostile? Nurturing or disparaging? Stagnating or full of opportunities?

- Do the images in the media and advertising have too much influence on how you feel and think about yourself and others?

- Is your perspective one of optimism, pessimism, or, what I call, optimistic realism?

  ➢ Do you look exclusively for the positives or is your focus centered on the negatives? *Or*, do you "see" both sides, hoping for the best but preparing for the worst?

> Do you think in terms of "all good" or "all bad" (black & white thinking)?

> Do you believe people are born with certain talents, skills and abilities that are "fixed?" Or, do you believe that people can "grow," learning new ones and improving on the ones they already possess?

- Do you have an internal or external locus of control?

> Internal – you feel empowered to make decisions that affect your life

> External – you feel like forces outside of yourself determine how your life will be

What kind of Mindset do you have?

- A "healthy" mindset (internal locus of control; empowered & focused on a healthy lifestyle; positive & growth-oriented)

- A "skinny" mindset (external locus of control; overly influenced by media images; perfectionistic; "black & white" thinking; negative)

- A "helpless" mindset (external locus of control; "fixed;" think there is no point in trying to make changes; lacking in self-worth; negative)

The mindset you adopt ultimately determines if any changes you make will be effective and long-lasting.

Breaking out of a negative mindset, filling your toolbox with a variety of effective, healthy coping skills, and changing your beliefs about yourself, food, and how you perceive your body are positive actions you can take to revise your relationship with food, yourself, and the world around you. These positive actions provide the building blocks for a healthy lifestyle that provides you with the energy and motivation to pursue your passions and life goals.

Love yourself enough to adopt a healthy mindset that supports you in living a healthy lifestyle.

Chapter Three:

RESETTING YOUR RELATIONSHIP WITH FOOD & YOUR BODY

"Once you begin to see that your relationship with food is a doorway, then you can truly begin the process of healing and transformation."

psychologyofeating.com

Breaking free from disordered eating patterns and a poor body image requires making a major mindset shift on how you look at your eating difficulties. By making this paradigm shift, you can:

◆ Find freedom from shame, frustration, guilt, depression, anxiety, and self-hatred.

◆ Transform your relationship with food and your body.

Regardless of what you've tried in the past (diet, exercise, etc.), not shifting your perspective will keep you "stuck" in your negative eating patterns or susceptible to relapsing into old habits and coping strategies. Making the necessary mindset shift is more easily accomplished by accessing the creative part of your brain rather than staying entrenched in using the analytical part of your brain.

Look at the lines above. At first, they appear to be two parallel lines with a dotted line in the middle. But, what happens when I say "See the two lane highway? " Your perception immediately shifts and you see a different meaning to the lines. You've gained a new perspective. This is one example of how shifting how you think about something can shift how you perceive it. Making these types of mental shifts will help you look at your disordered eating in an entirely different way.

Individuals who suffer from a disordered pattern of eating may see food and eating as the problem. But, since food is a necessary component to survive, it cannot simply be "given up" or replaced with an alternative. This creates a dilemma that's difficult to solve even though there are a multitude of options for solving it – dieting, fasting, exercising to compensate, weight loss pills and supplements, etc. If you're one of these individuals, you know that these strategies can work in the short term, but often cannot be sustained over time and they do not focus on health.

What if, however, a mental shift took place that helped you "see" your disordered eating differently? What if you were able to see your disordered eating as an attempt to solve deeper issues…as a coping strategy rather than as the problem itself? Sometimes, the key to permanently solving a problem is to shift your perspective on it. You can do this more effectively if you access the creative side of your brain through the use of imagery, metaphors, and stories. The following example highlights what I mean. It can get you thinking and feeling differently about your situation and how to go about changing it.

Look at the illustration below and imagine that you're the individual on the island. You've been stranded there for months, maybe even years. You feel hopeless and helpless to change your situation. You want off the island, but you're swimming skills aren't strong enough to get you very far. Staying on the island keeps you alive, but your health is deteriorating and your underlying problem hasn't gone away. One day, you spot a boat in the distance and immediately "see" it as your salvation – the answer to all of your problems.

Now, shift your perspective to the individual floating rudderless in the open water. You've been stuck on the boat for so long that you've lost track of time. You feel out of control of your destination and lack the tools to navigate or steer the boat. You feel hopeless and helpless. Staying in the boat keeps you alive, but forces outside of yourself control where you end up. Then, you spy a small island on the otherwise empty horizon and begin to rejoice. It appears to be the answer to your problems.

Each individual sees the other person's "problem" as the "solution" to theirs. Depending on how you choose to look at a situation, event, behaviour, or problem, it can change everything. A mental shift can open up possibilities, solutions, and a whole new way of "seeing" things. In reality, neither "solution" in this example is a long term one, but, if the individuals chose to support and help each other, they could come up with a way to permanently solve both of their underlying problems. Connection to supportive others, brainstorming, sharing resources, and learning new skills are all key pieces to going beyond physiological survival and getting our higher level needs met.

By focusing on food, eating, or weight other essential needs are masked and left unaddressed.

Think of your disordered eating as the island or the boat. They both provide short term "safety" and physiological survival, but in the long run they become part of the deeper problem of being lost at sea. By focusing on food, eating, or weight, other essentials needs are masked and left unaddressed. Only by viewing your disordered eating as a coping strategy that uses food as a distraction and comfort from emotionally distressing problems can you begin to uncover these unmet needs and determine how best to deal with them directly. Left buried in your unconscious, these issues fester and negatively influence your ability to live a healthy and prosperous life.

Even though you may have initially been ill-equipped to deal with the real problem, once you've uncovered and clarified what it is, you can develop the necessary skills to resolve it. And, you don't have to do it alone...you can surround yourself with supportive, knowledgeable people who encourage and believe in you. This support network could include a combination of natural supports (friends, family, community groups, etc.) and professional supports (Mental Health Professional, Wellness or Recovery Coach, Nutritionist, etc.). The point is, you have the power to "see" your disordered eating differently. This new perspective allows you to take actions that will help you ditch your disordered eating and replace it with healthier coping strategies and live a happier, more authentic life.

A reoccurring theme found in women's accounts of their various struggles with eating is their heightened ability to "see" subtle realities others aren't sensitive enough to perceive. When they tried to express this reality, however, their perception was rejected, ignored, discounted, and ridiculed. Some women were even abused for expressing their perceptions. Their voice was stifled and they began doubting themselves, their instincts, and their intuition.

Over time, these women became convinced that there was something inherently wrong with them and they began desperately searching for a way to "fit in," confusing "fitting in" with belonging. They began acting as though they thought, felt, and "saw" things like everyone else did. Ultimately, they abandoned their true selves in an attempt to meet their overwhelming need to belong. (More on this in Chapter 5.)

THE TRUTH: There is nothing wrong with being emotionally sensitive, but there is something terribly wrong with an environment that makes individuals feel that way. Unable to control the situation they were born into or their innate sensitivity, and uneducated in the skills necessary to survive in an invalidating environment, many women turn to disordered eating behaviors to cope with their internal struggle.

Looked at through this mental lens, disordered eating can be viewed as an attempt to fill the emotional emptiness, loneliness and powerful longing created by this fundamental disconnection from others and the misguided desire to "fit in." Unfortunately it also results in disconnecting from their true selves and having shallow relationships with others. When the authentic self is lost, real intimacy and deep connections are impossible to obtain.

"The Truth is: Belonging starts with self-acceptance. Your level of belonging, in fact, can never be greater than your level of self-acceptance, because believing that you're enough is what gives you the courage to be authentic, vulnerable and imperfect."

Brene´ Brown

How does food figure in to all of this?

When this quest to belong becomes confused and entangled with the desire to fit in, the pressure mounts to look and feel a certain way. You believe that you must only feel confident, secure, and successful. You believe that you must look like the cultural ideal – thin and beautiful. And, if this is not your natural body shape or appearance, you must diet, modify, and/or exercise your body into submission. Consequently, food takes on a new meaning and function in your life.

But – your body was designed to protect you, even against yourself. It will do everything in its power to be sure that your basic survival needs are met. That's why dieting doesn't work in the long run.

Imagine that you're driving home from work and you're starving. On the physical hunger scale you're at a "2." Maybe you had a hectic day and skipped lunch or you're on a strict diet that's left you feeling hungry and deprived. As you travel down the street, what catches and holds your attention? Are you focused on your driving, aware of pedestrians and the vehicles coming and going? Not hardly! Your attention is captured by...

...every restaurant and every fast food place you pass with their beckoning signs, delicious aromas and colorful, larger than life images of tempting food choices ranging from big, juicy cheeseburgers to spicy, tantalizing tacos.

Why? Because your body is specifically designed to help you physiologically survive – to get you thinking about food and how to get it. And, if you don't pay attention to your body's subtle cues, it will turn up the volume and intensity...forcing you to take actions that promote your survival.

If you're on a diet, you're going to be thinking about all the foods you're not supposed to have because that's the way your brain is designed. If I say "pay no attention to the chocolate cake on the table in front of you," what are you going to think about? You might be able to shift your attention temporarily, but before long, the rebel inside you will turn your attention repeatedly to the delicious looking layer cake even if you avoid looking at it.

Now, imagine that on top of this, you have a conflicted relationship with your father, your boyfriend just cheated on you, you just moved and are having difficulty making friends, or your workplace is hostile and unrewarding. You're faced with both types of hunger – physical and emotional. It's easy to get confused and believe that the comfort of food is the answer to both problems.

The second set of problems, however, require a more complex skill set to solve and you may be ill-equipped to deal with them. If you grew up in an emotionally insensitive and invalidating environment, it's unlikely that you learned the necessary skills from your family, friends, television, movies, or at school. So, you shift your focus to the less complicated problem with the simpler "solution" - the fat on your body, your weight, your appearance. Your other problems are shoved out of your conscious awareness, unattended to and negatively impacting your happiness and ability to live a full and authentic life.

Your world begins to revolve around food rather than food being fuel and a source of non-guilty pleasure. Food is no longer just food, it's become a symbol for deeper issues and disordered eating becomes your "go-to" method of coping. It becomes a distraction and a way of self-medicating to emotionally numb yourself.

Life Preserver Metaphor

Imagine yourself on the deck of a small, pitching boat in the middle of a raging storm. You're barely managing to keep your balance when an especially big wave slams into the boat and you lose your balance, falling into the water. It's impossible to climb back into the boat. As you splash frantically in the choppy water, you can see the shore in the distance, but you're not a very skilled swimmer. Your survival instinct kicks in and you grab hold of a life preserver that floats by to keep yourself from drowning.

Clinging to the life preserver keeps your head above water during the storm, but, eventually, you reach calmer waters and try to paddle your way to shore. You paddle and you paddle but you can't seem to get any closer because you're still clinging to the life preserver. The irony is that the very thing that saved your life during the storm is now getting in the way of you getting where you want to be in life.

The life preserver is your disordered eating. It's served a very important function in your life, but now you need to figure out exactly what that function is....

To make things even tougher, there's always some well-meaning person standing on the shore yelling "let go of the life preserver, let go of the life preserver," and it makes you feel weak and stupid because you can't let go. The harder they push for you to "just let go," the more scared and resistant you feel.

It's time to make another very important mental shift. Letting go of your life preserver may not be your best course of action. There's a very wise part of you that won't let you let go until you're good and ready – until you've become a more skilled swimmer. If you let go of the life preserver and start swimming toward shore without the necessary skills you may not have the strength, stamina, or confidence to make it all the way and you'd probably drown. You'd be too far from shore and too far from the life preserver.

There is, however, another option. You can let go of the life preserver with one hand and try floating. When you need to, you can grab back on with both hands. Then, you can try treading water or paddling and, when you get tired, grab back on and rest for a while. This isn't failure, it's progress! You can do this as many times as you need to until you have the strength, confidence, and skills necessary to make it all the way to solid ground. Once you make it to the shore you can let go of the life preserver completely because it no longer serves a function in your life. You've learned how to swim and you don't need it anymore.

If you don't figure out the underlying issues you'll keep looking for the answers to your problems in all the wrong places, remaining frustrated and trapped in a cycle of self-loathing and animosity toward your body. You'll continue to believe that there's something wrong with you for not being able to break free from your disordered eating patterns and negative body image.

You must "decipher" your eating behavior and what food symbolizes to you to discover what its true function is.

A Little Motivational Exercise

Describe what your life will be like in 3 years if you continue to cling to your eating disorder. Be specific, even if the vision scares you.

_____

_____

_____

_____

Now, describe what your life would be like without your disordered eating? Be specific...it's the vision of your potential future!

_____

_____

_____

_____

WHICH VISION WOULD YOU RATHER HAVE BECOME YOUR REALITY???

In order to make the second vision of your future reality, transform your relationship with food and your body by learning to decipher what the food itself represents. Once you learn the hidden meaning in the foods you crave, you'll be able to eat with mindful intention, make desired changes that will last, and learn the specific skills you need to confront and address the problems that create your emotional hunger.

In the past you may have encountered obstacles, including self-sabotaging your own efforts to break free from disordered eating. Maybe you've been able to stick to a restrictive diet for an extended period of time only to become overwhelmed by feelings of deprivation and the urge to binge. Perhaps you thought "I've been extremely good lately, it's okay if I cheat just a little" and then lost control of your eating.

This doesn't mean you're hopeless and weak – it means your normal! Slips like these are normal because our brains don't like to be told to *just NOT do something* that feels or tastes good or relieves our stress and anxiety. The insistent voice in our head that supports disordered eating has been called our "inner rebel." We all have one and she doesn't react well when her needs and desires aren't being met. We can talk back to her for a while, keeping her under wraps, but when we're feeling exhausted, emotionally stressed, or distracted, she rises up in rebellion and takes control of our thoughts and behavior.

The only way to quiet your inner rebellious voice is to discover what it is that you (and your inner rebel) are REALLY hungry for and deal with it directly. The food you choose may provide clues to discovering what this is. Your food choice can indicate the type of emotions you're experiencing. The next chapter is a guide for deciphering the messages hidden in your food choices and will help you uncover your unconscious emotions and unmet needs.

Chapter Four:

What's The Hidden Message In Your Food Craving?

"Food for the body is not enough. There must be food for the soul."

Dorothy Day

The need to feel comforted and fulfilled is universal and often leads many of us to turn to food to supply these feelings. It's a coping strategy many of us are unwittingly taught in childhood. We may have fond memories pairing food with love.   Food can provide quick relief from discomfort, but unfortunately, that relief is only temporary and ultimately reinforces disordered eating patterns. If the strategy is utilized frequently enough it becomes our "life preserver. "

For long lasting relief it's necessary to explore, express, and deal with the root cause of unpleasant emotions and vague feelings of discontent, otherwise, the underlying issue gets buried deeper inside and further from awareness. Paying attention to food cravings can lead to discovering needs that aren't being satisfied and a path to solving the real issues (ones that you may not have identified yet) your disordered eating is masking. Craving certain types of food can be an indicator of what is really troubling you.

Deciphering the Hidden Messages in Your Food

One of the ways you can discover what's really going on and

needs to be addressed directly and proactively is to get curious about the foods you crave. The following food description exercise provides insight that may surprise you. It can uncover feelings and problems you haven't acknowledged or recognized until now.

What Can I Learn From My Food?

Begin the exercise by asking yourself:

What food would I choose if I could eat as much of it as I want without any negative consequences?

_____

Now, describe that food as if you were describing it to someone who has never had it before. Go into detail about the qualities of that food – not the fat content or calorie count, but the taste, texture, aroma.

Is it smooth, creamy, and sweet? Crunchy, salty, and noisy to eat? Is it spicy enough to make your eyes water? Is it soft, chewy and filling? Does it smell like your grandmother's kitchen on Saturday mornings?

_____

_____

_____

_____

_____

Include any memories (good or bad) you have that are
associated with this particular food or ones that are similar.

_____

_____

_____

_____

_____

What feelings come up when you think about this food?

_____

_____

_____

_____

What thoughts arise as you do this exercise?

_____

_____

_____

_____

_____

Summarize what you've learned about your cravings so far:

_____

_____

_____

_____

To further your path of discovery, here are some commonly associated emotions/needs that correlate with general cravings that can help you decipher the hidden message in your food choices, some questions to explore, and a few non-food related suggestions to try:

Sweets: a lack of joy and/or sweetness in life; feeling exhausted and running on empty

- If the everyday grind has worn you down, in what ways can you add sweetness & joy back into your life?
- Incorporate 30 minutes of fun activity into your day.

Salty: stress, anger, frustration, anxiety; a desire to relax and unwind

- What do I feel stressed, anxious, or angry about?
- How can I deal with these situations directly and assertively?
- Reflect on your life and how you can "go with the flow", do something that relaxes you like deep breathing, going for a run, yoga, etc.

Spicy: boredom; wanting more joy and excitement in life; wanting to increase creativity and intuition; wanting to feel more physically awake and alive

- If you're feeling bored, restless, or discontent with your situation, think of ways that you can "spice" up your life.
- What small, healthy changes can you make that will make you feel more alive?

Soft & Chewy: feeling mixed emotions; wanting hugs and affection; needing comfort and sustenance

- Where do you need extra comfort?
- What seems to be hard in your life right now?
- What are some healthy ways you can keep yourself moving forward through the hard stuff?
- Try talking to a friend, joining a support group, enlisting professional help, etc.

Crunchy: indicates "hard" emotions that are directed outward – anger, bitterness, frustration, resentment, stress and/or tension; feeling the desire to lash out

- What or who do you want to "crush" in your life?
- Are you feeling misunderstood, pressured, or abused in any way?
- What or who would you really like to chew on?
- Will that chip, cracker, or cookie change your situation?
- What can you do that will? Brainstorm solutions and take assertive action.

Soft & Creamy: indicates "soft" emotions that are directed inward – self-directed anger, betrayal, embarrassment, fear, grief, insecurity, regret, sadness, self-doubt, shame, emptiness, loneliness, depression; a deep longing for comfort or reassurance

- ♦ If you don't know what it is that you want, ask yourself "What's missing in my life?"
- ♦ Don't stop with the obvious answer, dig deeper. Then look for ways to provide what's missing for yourself that don't include food.
- ♦ Find ways to heal your pain rather than mask it or stuff it down inside.

High Fat Foods: fear of facing something

- ♦ Identify your fear and face it head on. Only by facing it, can you reduce its power and begin to find a resolution. Sometimes the things we fear the most are the things we most need to do.

Caffeine: feeling weighed down by unwanted responsibilities or stuck in a job that doesn't suit you; wanting to feel more awake and alive on a mental level and to concentrate

- ♦ If you're feeling put upon, drained, and unfulfilled in your job give yourself a mental break, get more rest, set firmer boundaries, and explore new job opportunities that correspond with your natural interests.
- ♦ Just because you're good at something doesn't mean you love doing it! Figure out a way to do what you love, don't focus on the reasons you can't.

Chocolate: feeling unloved; wanting romance, to feel good and in-love; needing more intimacy

- Think about the love in your life: Where do you have it? Where is it missing?
- What can you do to create more love and intimacy in your life?
- Remember that your ability to give and receive love begins with your ability to love yourself first. Practice the art of Self Love. (not to be confused with narcissism)

Ice Cream: feeling emotionally hurt; wanting to freeze painful feelings, coat them with something soothing, and feel good and carefree

- What's hurting?
- What would you like to be free from?
- List all of the ways you can think of that you feel carefree & free in your daily life – go for a bike ride, run, or nature walk; take a warm soothing bath or other nurturing activity that helps heal your emotional wounds.
- Engage in non-food related self-care activities that nourish your soul.

Cheese: feeling the need to be emotionally nourished, physically and emotionally "mothered"; desire to feel grounded, comforted and cared for

- What's missing in your life?
- To feel more supported and connected, find a community or personal "tribe" that makes you feel safe to express yourself honestly and you can connect with in a deep and meaningful way.

- ♦ Surround yourself with people who appreciate you for who you are, support self-growth, and lift you up.
- ♦ Limit your exposure to people who are "toxic" to your feelings of well-being.

Food Aroma Clues

The way a food smells may also provide clues to what you're seeking or an emotion you'd like to generate. Think about the food smells that you're most drawn to. Which ones make you feel loved? Which ones do you shun? Some of this is personal preference of course, but some of the draw comes from memories associated with those specific foods.

The examples listed are common food aroma associations, but they might not necessarily "fit" for you, depending on your history and your experiences with them. Try to imagine each smell, or, better yet, find something that has that aroma and use it to help stimulate your senses. For example, peppermint gum, a piece of chocolate, vanilla extract, an orange, strawberry preserves, Mexican food or cinnamon.

What feeling does each food aroma evoke? What memories are stimulated? What thoughts come up as you inhale each smell?

Peppermint: boosts energy, stamina & mental clarity
Chocolate: generates feelings of being loved
Vanilla: generates happy & relaxed feelings
Citrus: stimulates & energizes the mind & body
Strawberry: enhances motivation to get "moving" physically
Orange: refreshes & relaxes
Spicy: generates feelings of excitement & energy

What food aromas generate a strong emotional reaction for you? List both pleasant and unpleasant ones and identify what you associate them with.

_____

_____

_____

_____

_____

_____

_____

Raising your awareness of the reasons you're eating and why you choose the foods that you do will help you unlock the mystery of your disordered eating and determine the skills you need to start letting go. When you recognize that you're eating for emotional reasons rather than physical hunger, you can choose a healthy replacement. The next chapter provides more non-food related alternatives.

Chapter Five

Identifying Your Unmet Needs

"The only person who can meet your unmet needs – from childhood or the present – is you."

Hannah Braime

Basic Human Needs

In 1943 Abraham Maslow, an American Psychologist, proposed a motivational theory based on a 5 tier model of human needs. He postulated that people are motivated to have certain needs met and that some of these needs take precedence over others. According to this theory, the most basic need is physical survival (food, water, shelter, etc.). The next higher tier is the need for safety and security (order, law, stability, protection, etc.).

Once these basic needs are met, psychological needs of belongingness (acceptance, intimacy, trust, friendship, affiliation with a group, giving and receiving love) and esteem (achievement, mastery, self-esteem, status, responsibility, etc.) can be focused on. Finally, at the top of the Maslow's original needs hierarchy is self-actualization (achieving one's full potential, personal growth, and creative activity).

In the 1960's, this model was expanded to include cognitive needs (curiosity, acquisition of knowledge and understanding, seeking meaning and purpose), aesthetic needs (seeking and appreciating beauty, balance, etc.), and transcendence needs (helping others to reach self-actualization).

The expanded needs hierarchy suggests that human needs fall into the following order of importance:

1. **Biological and Physiological Needs**

-   air, water, food, clothing, shelter

2. **Safety Needs**

-   personal & financial security, health & well-being

3. **Love and Belongingness Needs**

-   friendship, intimacy, family, being an integral part of a group

-   to love and be loved – both sexually & non-sexually

4. **Esteem Needs**

-   respect, self-esteem & self-respect, status, recognition, acceptance & feeling valued, strength, attention, independence, confidence, competence, mastery, freedom

5. Cognitive Needs

- knowledge, understanding, curiosity, exploration, meaning, predictability

6. Aesthetic Needs

- appreciation & search for beauty, balance, etc.

7. Self-Actualization Needs

- realizing personal potential, self-fulfillment, personal growth, experiences

8. Transcendence Needs

- altruism & helping others reach for self-actualization

The motivation to have these needs met is now considered to be pluralistic in nature – the drive to meet multiple needs can be operating at once. You might be motivated by higher growth needs at the same time as more basic needs. Don't make the mistake of believing that just because you might be struggling to find appropriate housing and/or a job that provides financial security that you can't be struggling with the need to belong, to love and to be loved or for esteem, self-actualization, cognitive, aesthetic, or transcendence needs at the same time.

Your mission is to uncover all of your unmet needs as they arise so that you can problem solve each, identify and learn necessary skills you may be lacking, and empower yourself to deal with your unmet needs directly rather than masking them with the distraction of food, weight issues, or appearance.

Although some needs will take precedence over others at times, to successfully ditch your disordered eating permanently, you cannot neglect your higher order needs. Changes in the importance and satisfaction of needs is relative to your current circumstances. Understanding this can help you pinpoint what might be missing in your life right now...or six months from now. Chances are, the answer may be different.

The Need to Belong

One of the needs that plays a major role in disordered eating is the need to belong and feel a strong, deep connection to others...to be part of a family, a community, a tribe or group of like-minded people. This sense of belonging is not fulfilled by merely fitting in with the crowd. It's about being accepted and appreciated for your unique qualities, not outward appearances or your willingness to acquiesce without question to the ideas and dictates of a few. A sense of belonging comes from being valued and "seen" for who you truly are. The ability to remain connected and true to your authentic self while you connect with others is the foundation for feeling that you belong, not like an imposter desperately hoping your "secrets" won't be discovered.

If the hunger to belong gets confused with the hunger for food, then food becomes seen as the problem. And because the hunger to belong never goes away, your "appetite" can't be satisfied regardless of how much food you consume. Learning to accept your flaws, the things about yourself that aren't perfect and you're not great at, allows you to value and appreciate yourself as a whole – unique, beautifully imperfect, and infinitely human. This all-encompassing self-acceptance gives you the freedom to be yourself and the ability to forge authentic connections with others that are mutually satisfying.

The Need for Esteem

The need for esteem can be looked at as having two components: self esteem and the esteem of others. The need to have the esteem and respect of others is reflected in the desire to be accepted and valued by others and includes gaining recognition, status, fame, prestige, and attention. The need for self esteem and self respect is reflected in the desire for inner strength, competence, self confidence, mastery, independence, and freedom.

Both esteem components are necessary to satisfy the need for esteem. But, it's difficult to feel the esteem of others if you don't have esteem for yourself first. Feeling confident in yourself and your abilities gives you the courage to put yourself out there, to take on tasks that bring status, fame, and recognition. Respecting yourself and pursuing things you're passionate about naturally brings you attention and respect from others.

Identifying Your Unmet Needs

To begin to identify and heighten your awareness of your unmet needs, start by asking yourself "What's missing in my life right now?" If the answer isn't obvious or is too vague, continue your exploration with these specific needs related questions:

- Are my basic survival needs being met?

- Do I feel safe, both emotionally and physically?

- Am I struggling to feel a sense of belonging?

- Do I feel valued and loved?

- Are my efforts and abilities recognized and appreciated by myself and others?

- Do I feel intellectually stimulated and open to new ideas?

- Do I feel in or out of control of my life?

- Is there beauty and balance in my life?

- Am I engaging in self-growth activities that will help me become the best version of myself?

- Do I encourage and help others to reach their full potential?

Summarize the unmet need(s) you've been able to identify:

_____

_____

_____

_____

How are these unmet needs reflected in your disordered eating?

_____

_____

_____

_____

It's important to note that your needs are interrelated, not sharply divided into distinct and separate categories. As you can see, satisfying the need for esteem *and* the need to belong and reciprocate love both require feeling respected, valued and accepted for all the parts that make you, uniquely you.

Once your unmet needs have been identified, you can develop a plan to address them and learn the necessary skills you need to do so. One of these skills is substituting healthier coping strategies or tools for your disordered eating that directly address your unmet needs. The next chapter takes a closer look at how you can do this.

Chapter Six:

Non-Food Replacement Toolbox

If you find yourself in a hole, the first thing to do is stop digging. The second...find a way to climb out.

Imagine your unhappiness about your life, your weight, and your body as a "hole" that you're stuck in. Imagine that food is the "shovel" in your hand and "digging" is your disordered eating. The longer you've been trying to "dig" your way out of your unhappiness, the deeper the hole is and the harder it is to see the bright blue sky and freedom.

What happens if you keep using food and disordered eating to deal with your unhappiness? The hole just gets deeper and deeper – the feelings of helplessness, hopelessness, and depression grow along with the size of the hole.

Now, imagine that you decide to stop digging, set the shovel aside (but not too far in case you need it), and try different tools and/or approaches to solving your unhappiness problem. Ones that help you to climb out of the hole. Each healthy, empowering replacement tool you use will help you carve another step that leads up and out of the hole. Each step getting you closer and closer to ditching your disordered eating for good.

Is the climb easy? No. Will you slip and need the shovel sometimes? Yes. Will you reach the top and freedom? Yes...as long as you don't give up on yourself and you keep choosing healthy alternatives more and more frequently.

Change is scary...even when the change is a positive and healthy one. Your feelings about making a change may be conflicted. Letting go of something that has helped you survive in the past can be terrifying at the same time that the promise of a freer, happier, healthier future without it is exhilarating.

Another reason you may be resistant to change is because you're focused on what you're giving up instead of focusing on what you have to gain. It can be helpful to make two different pros and cons lists to shift your focus to all the great things you could have if you take the steps necessary to ditch your disordered eating and reset your relationship with food, yourself, and your body. Then go one step further, and make a detailed commitment to yourself.

It's not enough to just say that you want to get healthier, you have to be willing to do what it takes to make that happen!

Writing Exercise: To Ditch or Not to Ditch...That is the Question

Write down what's good about maintaining your disordered eating (pros) and what's bad about keeping it (cons). Then make another pros and cons list that details what's good about ditching your disordered eating (pros) and what's bad about giving it up (cons). Sometimes looking at the same problem from two different directions can provide even greater insight and motivation to make difficult changes.

When you're done with these lists, be thorough, summarize what you've learned and write a commitment statement to yourself that describes what you want to do differently and why.

Keeping Disordered Eating Pros & Cons

Pros	Cons

Ditching Disordered Eating Pros & Cons

Pros	Cons

Summarize what you've learned: _____

_____

_____

_____

_____

Write a specific, detailed commitment statement to yourself that describes changes you want to make, why you want to make them, and what your goal is.

_____

_____

_____

Rewrite your commitment statement on a separate piece of paper. Mount it on your refrigerator or hang it up in another prominent place. Repeat your commitment to yourself several times a day. (My recommendation is to make this statement into a work of art – even if that art is generated on the computer. If you find pleasure in looking at it, the promise to yourself will carry even more impact.)

Now that you've made a strong commitment to change, to stop digging and put down the shovel...

What tool(s) can you pick up instead???

Ask any person who builds or restores things and they'll tell you that any restoring, remodeling, renovating or construction job is much easier and more successful when the right tools are available for each step of the process. Imagine trying to build a house with only a hammer or painting a picture with only one color of paint and an all-purpose paintbrush. A masterpiece can only be created if the artist has the right tools in their personal toolbox.

In this case, the *masterpiece* is a meaningful, joyous, and authentic life, the *artist* is you, and the *tools* are healthy non-food replacements and essential empowerment skills (interoceptive awareness, assertive communication, media literacy, emotional intelligence skills, self care skills) that enhance your ability to get your needs met satisfactorily.

Non-food Replacements to Add to Your Toolbox

Nonfood replacements include any activity that's healthy and meets the need being expressed in your negative thoughts and uncomfortable emotions. Whenever you're trying to change an unhealthy behavior, it's important to have a variety of healthy alternatives that you can replace it with. Replacement tools can be chosen to target physical, mental, or emotional needs. Depending on your unique set of needs, some tools will prove to be more or less effective for you. Ultimately, you want to fill your toolbox full of ones that suit you, that you're willing to use, and that work well for you.

(Noting the effectiveness of tools you've used in your Food Relationship Journal in Chapter 9 provides you with valuable information on what's working and what's not.)

Your choice of replacement behavior or activity will depend on your specific need, timing, available resources, and the parameters of the situation. For instance, even though you may desperately be in need of a hug and a shoulder to cry on, it may not be realistic to ask this of a co-worker nor do you want to inhale the chocolate covered doughnuts calling insistently from the break room – instead, you might give yourself some quiet time, take some deep breaths, and repeat some nurturing self-affirmations until you can visit your mother for that warm and nurturing hug and a safe space you're craving to express and release your vulnerable emotions.

Here's another replacement scenario: You had a stressful work day – cranky customers, short staffed, and low inventory. You spent most of your time addressing customer complaints and dealing with one crisis after another, leaving little time to take care of your personal needs. In fact, you didn't even have time for a lunch break. To top that off, you were promoted to shift manager 3 months ago, but only received a 15 cent raise.

You're STARVING! You're feeling unappreciated, resentful, and emotionally and physically drained. Your drive home takes you past a multitude of fast food places. You suddenly find yourself craving a double bacon cheeseburger and salty fries....

This is the perfect storm for disordered eating: You're physically hungry *and* you're emotionally hungry! You've gone too long without fueling your body and your need to be appreciated and valued is not being acknowledged or met.

What do you do???

First, take a deep breath. Ask yourself what you really need and want. Do you want to fuel your body with nutritious energy or junk? Do you want to feel great about taking care of yourself or disappointed for stuffing or distracting yourself food? Do you need a hug and words of recognition and specific praise? Do you need to rest, work off frustrations, or connect with a supportive friend?

Once you've answered these questions, you can make a decision that is informed and aware. You may choose to continue driving home, fix a protein packed salad for dinner, and then soak in a luxurious bath infused with eucalyptus and lavender before ending your evening by calling a friend who always makes you feel upbeat and valued.

Or, you may still choose to indulge in the bacon cheeseburger, but, you will have done so mindfully and by conscious choice rather than mindlessly and impulsively. Meaning, you're less likely to overeat and feel guilty or ashamed of your food choice later. You will satisfy your physical hunger, but then you will still need to proactively do something to satisfy your deeper emotional hunger for appreciation and acknowledgment. You still need to fill up your "emotional tank" with soul food. If you neglect to do this, this unmet need will continue to lurk in your unconscious and drive future food cravings.

Removing comfort foods will not cure your emotional hunger, you have to learn to comfort yourself.

Here is a general list of possible emotional eating replacement options:

- Move – engage in physical activity of some kind (from going down the hall to consult a co-worker to going for a run after work); the objective is to shift the energy in your body and move through your craving

- Listen to uplifting or calming music – steer clear from music that deepens your negative mood

- Get some fresh air – even if it's opening a window or taking a short walk around the block

- Read something entertaining or inspirational

- Take several slow, deep breaths; visualize breathing in positivity and breathing out negativity

- Play with or stroke a pet

- Visualize your happy place and spend some time there

- Review your goals & adjust if needed

- Recite an empowering and/or calming mantra

- Squeeze a stress ball or do some progressive relaxation

Your choices of healthy, non-food replacement activities or exercises is only limited by your imagination. Take a few minutes at the end of this chapter to write up a personalized list of ones that have worked well for you in the past or that you'd like to give a try. Keep this list in an easily accessible place to refer to if needed – being prepared before you're in crisis can be the difference between being happy or unhappy with the outcome.

You may want to make up separate lists for work, home, and outings with alternatives that are feasible for each specific location. What may work or be reasonable to use at home may not be appropriate for when you're out shopping or are stuck at work. You have the power to tailor when and where you use them to get the best possible outcome for you.

Some Self-Soothing & Calming Options

Aromatherapy

Aromatherapy is one alternative way to self-soothe and change your mood without reaching for food. Aromas activate the most primitive part of the brain called the limbic system. This is the part of the brain where we immediately experience emotions. There's a strong connection between smell, memory and mood. Smells can trigger memories and early associations that can either increase or decrease stress depending on the nature of the association (positive or negative). For this reason, it's important to pay attention to how aromas affect you.

For example, for one person the smell of fresh bread baking might evoke warm feelings and the memory of Saturday mornings spent with a loving grandmother. But, for someone else, the smell of baking bread might evoke grief and the memory of their grandmother dying of a heart attack while she was baking with them when they were 3 years old. As discussed earlier, aromas can have a huge impact on how we feel.

Here are a few aromatherapy options that might prove beneficial for you:

- Jasmine - relaxing, soothing, & confidence building

- Ylang Ylang – calming nerves, soothing, enhancing sensuality, decreasing depression and reducing frustration

- Sandalwood – promoting deep relaxation, decreasing depression, and quieting the mind & emotions, grounding

- Eucalyptus – comforting when feeling exhausted

- Lavender – calming & balancing

- Basil – uplifting, refreshing, clarifying, & aiding concentration

- Frankincense – relaxing, rejuvenating, dispelling fears

- Rose – soothing, sensual, confidence building

Suggestions for alleviating specific emotional states:

- Anger – chamomile, rose, ylang ylang

- Anxiety – bergamot, geranium, lavender, neroli, basil

- Depression – bergamot, clary sage, patchouli, ylang ylang

- Fear – frankincense, lavender, sandalwood

- Grief – rose, chamomile

- Irritability – lavender, neroli, rose, ylang ylang

- Resentment – rose

- Stress – bergamot, lavender, neroli, rose, sandalwood

Here are some suggestions for generating specific emotional states:

- Balanced – sandalwood

- Focused – lemon, basil, rosemary

- Confident – frankincense, jasmine, cedarwood, sandalwood, bergamot, neroli, rose

- Grounded – sandalwood, cedarwood, patcholi

*Reference: "Practical Art of Aromatherapy: Create your own personalized beauty treatments and natural remedies" by Deborah Nixon.

Rocking

Rocking is another self-soothing option that is underutilized by the adult population for themselves. Rocking as a way to nurture and calm your overwrought nerves makes sense if you think about it. Babies are rocked to sleep and to calm them when they're upset. Couples rock together on front porch swings to connect and unwind after a long day. In the olden days, women rocked by the fire, knitting or mending for their loved ones after a physically exhausting (and most probably thankless) day. Autistic children rock their bodies back and forth to soothe themselves and shut out the overload of outside stimulation.

When was the last time you sat down in a rocking chair or on a porch swing with no other purpose than to relax and give yourself a physical break from the day's hustle and bustle and a mental break from the day's worries?

**A personal note: This strategy only works for me if I'm the one in control of the rocking motion...hmmm...I'll let you come to your own conclusion on whether or not "being in control" is one of my underlying issues.

Self-Massage

Self-massage can serve many nurturing and soothing functions. It can provide relief from physical tension and sore muscles. It can be used in combination with aromatic essential oils for a calming effect. It can also be used to self nurture when the human need to be touched isn't being met in other healthy ways. And, it can be a means of accepting, loving, and reconnecting with your body.

**As a runner and author, I can vouch for using a foam roller or tennis ball as an aid to work out your kinks and relax muscle knots whether they're caused by the stress of deadlines and sitting for extended periods at the computer or doing a long and arduous hill run.

Take a Mini Reading Vacation

Taking a mini reading vacation provides you with a way to take a mental vacation from cognitive stress and the grind of everyday life. Pick a novel that's engaging and transports you to another time and place. Or pick one that's inspirational and taps into your "feel good" emotions. Your goal is to reduce your stress level and generate pleasant emotions to replace negative ones and the urge to soothe "raw" emotional edges by covering them up with food.

**If you're like me, however, you may need to set a time limit on your mini reading vacation. Otherwise, your stress relieving choice might prove to be counterproductive if you neglect your basic need for adequate sleep by staying up until 3 a.m. to finish reading it!

Yoga

Yoga is a great activity for reconnecting with yourself and your body. One of the really great things about practicing yoga is that you can pick poses or routines to target specific issues – relaxation, physical ailments, balance – both emotional and physical, connecting with and appreciating your body, building mental and physical strength, and so on.

**You can develop your own routine(s) that meet your particular needs. You can practice yoga virtually anywhere and you don't need fancy clothes or expensive equipment. I have different routines for strength building, recovery from hard workouts or runs, relaxation and de-stressing, and reconnecting with myself. I use *all* of the routines to listen to and respect my body and my inner wisdom.

Meditation

Meditation can be used to center and refocus yourself on the important things in your life, letting the insignificant annoyances float away. One useful meditation technique is to *Meditate on Nothing.* Meditating on nothing means to merely witness your thoughts. It's the act of allowing your thoughts to pass through your mind without latching onto or attaching a value to any of them.

Find a quiet, safe place where you won't be disturbed. Leave your electronic devices behind! Get comfortable, close your eyes, and take a few slow, deep, cleansing breaths.
Allow your thoughts to flow through your mind. Visualize them as text and merely watch them "float" by...don't allow yourself to judge them or hold on to them. If you're able to do so

successfully, you will provide yourself with proof that your thoughts only have power if you give it to them. Don't worry if you find yourself judging or following a train of thought...that's normal...simply remind yourself gently to let the thought go and bring yourself back to just noticing your thoughts as they pass through. You'll get better at it with practice.

Becoming masterful at *letting your thoughts go* enables you to give power to your positive thoughts while also being able to dis-empower your negative, self-defeating ones. Meditating on nothing also provides "distance" from your unpleasant thoughts and emotions. You can notice them without judging them. You can experience a calmness and clarity of thinking that allows you to gather insight into what lies beneath your troubling thoughts and emotions so that, later, you can brainstorm solutions.

*This tool & many others can be found in Mental Stress Management 2.0: 40 Tips For De-Cluttering Your "Inner Closet" & Emotional Stress Management 2.0: 40 Tips For Taming Your Turbulent Emotions.

Some Creative Options

Engaging in creative activities can be a powerful release for pent-up energy, emotions, and stress. The form and end-product of that creativity is not as important as how the process makes you feel...before, during and after you engage in the activity. Doing something creative can help met your need for more beauty and form in your life, your esteem needs by developing mastery of a technique or getting recognition for your work, and/or your need for self-actualization – expressed in paintings, a book, a photography portfolio, or an invention, etc.

<u>Artistic</u> – creating paintings, drawings, and/or collages can be a wonderful way to express your emotions, especially when they're difficult to verbalize.

<u>Hobbies & Crafts</u> – enjoy doing things you love that express who you are and provide another positive outlet for your emotions as well as a way to generate feelings of accomplishment and esteem.

<u>Writing</u> – express your emotions and creative side by journaling, writing poems, short stories, letters, etc. The end product doesn't have to be for anyone but you. The process of writing is a powerful form of expression that allows you to find your voice, clarify your feelings, and bring the unconscious into awareness.

<u>Refinishing Furniture</u> – there's something very therapeutic about lovingly restoring something that has been battered and worn by life into an even more beautiful version of itself that's only enhanced by its "scars."

Find a creative endeavor that feeds your soul and helps to relieve your tension and negative emotions...then, give yourself permission to spend time doing it!

Some Esteem Building Options

Esteem building tools are ones that develop self esteem, self confidence and feelings of achievement, self-respect and independence. They can also provide an avenue to gain the recognition of others.

Educate Yourself

Take a class (online or off), do some research on a topic that interests you or that you're struggling with, read self help books, and pursue other forms of education. Add to your knowledge base – knowledge gives you the power to make better decisions and be more in control of your life.

Master a New Skill

Learn and practice a new skill until you've reached mastery over it. It could be a life skill such as boundary setting or a physical skill such as shooting a free throw. Mastering new skills builds a sense of self confidence in one's ability to meet new challenges and is important to fulfill self-actualization needs.

Do Something You're Already Good At

Engaging in things that you're already good at strengthens feelings of confidence that provide a foundation for trying new things.

Some Stress Management Options

Feeling stressed is one of the most common triggers for disordered eating. To disrupt the stress eating cycle, it's important to identify the specific source of the stress and deal with it directly. This, however, may take time to sort out and the solutions to your stressors may take a while to implement, whereas your emotional hunger demands immediate attention. The other reality about stressors is that eliminating them may not be an option. That's why *everyone* needs to have a stress management plan that includes tools that can be used to alleviate both acute and chronic forms of stress.

Here is a sampling of stress management tools you can reach for instead of food:

Practice Gratitude

Take time to practice gratitude and remind yourself of what's truly important to you in your life. Grab a pen and paper instead of a snack. Write down at least 5 things that you're grateful for. As you do this, think about family and friends, health and safety, food and shelter, opportunities and freedoms, strengths and abilities. When you focus on what's truly important, the "buzz" in your head created by trivial things will grow quieter and you will feel calmer and more capable of taking on your challenges.

Pay Active Attention to Thoughts & Tasks You Want/Need to Focus On

A lot of tasks can be completed without much thought, leaving a lot of time to think about food. By paying active attention to the task at hand and to your accompanying thoughts, you can redirect those thoughts, channeling them to be more productive. Even the simplest of tasks can go awry if your mind is on other things, causing you added work and stress when they do.

In With the Good, Out With the Bad

This breathing exercise will help you to release tension and pent-up emotions in the moment and to calm your thoughts and emotions when they feel overwhelming. Focus on your breathing. Imagine breathing in clean, energizing calmness and breathing out toxic waves of tension. Imagine positive thoughts and feelings coming in as you inhale and self-defeating thoughts and feelings flowing out as you exhale. Do this until you feel calmer and more relaxed.

Create an Emotional Sanctuary

A sanctuary is a place of safety; a refuge. An "emotional sanctuary" is a place where you feel safe from harm (both physical and emotional) and free to express your emotions regardless of what they might be. Creating an emotional sanctuary means creating a space that allows you to let down your emotional guard and feel whatever you're feeling in that moment.

- Pick a space in your home that provides privacy and security – this may be a bedroom with a locked door.

- Organize it so it doesn't feel chaotic.

- Furnish it with soothing and comforting things – pillows, plush blankets, a huggable teddy bear, etc.

- Infuse the space with calming scents and paint it a soft color.

- Add any additional items that make you feel safe, secure, loved, and comforted – photo of your mother, mantras that soothe you, mementos of happy times, etc.

Curl up in this safe space whenever you need to feel nurtured, supported, and comforted. Allow yourself to embrace your emotions as they arise. Acknowledge them, name them, and let yourself experience them. Even though they might be overwhelming at first, know that like the waves in the ocean they will peak and then they will ebb. If you allow them to flow through you, the peaks will gradually decrease in size and intensity. Once this happens, you're in a much better state to learn from them, problem solve, and make important decisions about how you want to move forward.

For more stress management ideas, refer to The Stress Management 2.0 Series listed in the back of this book.

Keep in mind that some of the replacement options discussed in this chapter may satisfy more than one need. That makes them even more powerful and versatile tools to have in your toolbox.

Here are three of my favorite "tools" to clarify this point:

Running: mental distraction or problem solving; physical outlet for stress and strong emotions; self-care; reconnect with self and body; confidence and esteem building

Writing: creative outlet; emotional expression; way to organize thoughts or tasks; vehicle to self reflect without judging; achievement; transcendence

Baking: soothing; self care (baking nutritious food that tastes awesome); a way to show appreciation to others by gifting them with great tasting, good for them goodies; creative outlet; mastery

I've only just scratched the surface when it comes to alternative tools/options to replace food as your "go-to" coping strategy. You have an infinite number of tools to choose from, the important point to remember is to pick ones that are effective and realistic for you – ones that you're drawn to, not necessarily the ones that are easiest to implement.

You can start compiling your tools on the next page. The great thing about these tools – they can also translate into skills that will help you get your needs met on a regular basis and deal with your deeper issues directly and proactively.

Tools I Want to Add to My Toolbox

List the tools/options that you want to add to your coping toolbox to use instead of food. Add to the list over time. Delete ones that prove to be ineffective. Overhaul your toolbox from time to time – update tools as needed or when you find one that works better for your circumstances at that time.

1.

2.

3.

4.

5.

6.

7.

8.

9.

10.

11.

12.

"She stood in the storm, and when the wind did not blow her way, she adjusted her sails." Elizabeth Edwards

Chapter 7

Putting the Disordered Eating Puzzle Together

Instead of shying away from challenges and life's ups and downs, meet them head on with enthusiasm, courage and the determination to live life on your terms.

Empowerment skills are needed to navigate in a world that doesn't value, understand, or appreciate individuals who are emotionally sensitive and highly intuitive and for whom disordered eating has become a coping mechanism. Empowerment skills are life skills that build a foundation for operating from a position of personal power – assertive, aware, emotionally intelligent, self-accepting, and media literate. Each skill area contains sub-skills that can be learned, practiced, and mastered.

Remember back to when you were first learning to ride a bike. It took a few scrapes, bumps and even falling over before you were able to stay upright while you pedaled. But, you didn't give up. Your maiden rides were wobbly and lacked confidence, but, with practice and determination, you were eventually able to glide smoothly and confidently wherever you wanted to go, even when the terrain got rough or difficult.

The same process works when learning life skills. No one is an expert at first, but over time and with consistent practice and the motivation to live your life free of disordered eating, you can master empowerment skills that will serve you in all aspects of your life, not just your struggles with food, weight issues, and your relationship with your body.

Resetting your relationship with food requires making the decision to interrupt your disordered eating patterns, increase your awareness, address the underlying issues that the disordered eating is masking, and learn new skills to deal directly with difficult emotions and tough problems. It may feel like an impossible task – you may have even attempted it before, but it becomes less daunting and more "doable" when it's broken down into manageable pieces. Think of your disordered eating as a puzzle to be solved and the following tips as a guide to discovering and putting all the pieces of the puzzle together. The challenge to this resetting process is figuring out how the pieces can fit together in a new way. But, once you figure this out, the end result will create a very different picture!

Puzzle Piece #1: Decide you deserve it.

Building a healthy relationship with food is a process that takes time, but the first step is to make the decision that you want, need, and deserve to be accepted, valued and loved despite your flaws, past mistakes, or current circumstances. If you don't believe that you're worth it, any changes you make will be short-lived. Sooner or later, you'll self-sabotage your progress towards disordered eating recovery. A healthy relationship with food is part of achieving life fitness and living a physically, mentally, and emotionally healthy lifestyle.

Puzzle Piece #2: Raise Your Food Relationship Awareness

There are a lot of things you do throughout any given day that are done without conscious decision making. Eating may be one of those things. Consistently filling out a Food Relationship Journal or Notebook is a good way to bring your eating behaviors and what's driving them into your conscious awareness. A food relationship journal can provide valuable insight to help you identify eating triggers (events, emotions, etc.), clarify the function that food serves in your life – what deeper issues it represents, correctly interpret physiological hunger cues and differentiate between physical hunger and emotional hunger (interoceptive awareness), and identify the skills you need to develop in order to deal directly with problems that have previously felt too difficult or complicated to tackle. (More on this in Chapter 9.)

Puzzle Piece #3: Develop Essential Empowerment Skills

Once you've made the decision that you're worth the effort and have discovered the unconscious thoughts, feelings, and problems that are driving and supporting your disordered eating, you can determine what skills you need to effectively address these issues rather than avoiding them. I use the term "empowerment skills" because each skill empowers you to make different decisions and take control of your life in a conscious and deliberate way. Resetting your relationship with food requires mastering the following empowerment skills. As you review them, ask yourself: Which ones do I need to develop?

Essential Empowerment Skills:

Interoceptive Awareness – the awareness of your body's hunger and satiety cues (AA – appetite awareness) and the ability to recognize and correctly identify emotions (EA – emotional awareness). (More on this in Chapter 8.)

Assertive Communication – the ability to identify, accept, and express your feelings in a way that honors both your experience and the experience of others. Communicating assertively allows you to stand up for yourself without hurting others and you're more likely to get your needs met satisfactorily.

Media Literacy – understanding the truth behind advertising and the images portrayed in the media; questioning their validity and realizing that you're being "sold" an unrealistic standard of beauty and body appearance through manipulation, "smoke and mirrors," and making you feel bad about yourself, your body, and your status. (More on body image in Chapter 10.)

Emotional Intelligence – learning to control the expression of your emotions, not attempting to control the emotion itself; learning to listen to what your emotions are telling you – i.e. when to say "yes" and when to say "no," when to move forward cautiously and when to speed up, what to steer clear of and what to embrace, etc.

Self Care – taking care of yourself in all three life fitness domains: physical, mental, and emotional; using self-reflection to figure out what you most need (these needs may change from day to day, as circumstances change, or when a traumatic event occurs, etc.) and taking actions to provide it for yourself; healthy stress management and learning a variety of healthy coping skills and non-food self-soothing activities that work effectively for you.

Puzzle Piece #4: Replace Disordered Eating with Healthier Coping Options/Tools

Whenever you're trying to change an unhealthy behavior, it's important to have a variety of healthy alternatives that you can replace it with. Your choice of replacement will depend on the specific unmet need, timing, and situation. Once you've found ones that work well for you, you can undo unhealthy lifestyle habits that include disordered eating.

Being human, you are, by nature, a creature of habit. When you're exposed to different situations, you store information about that situation in your memory. The more often you're exposed to the same situation (i.e. eating to stuff down feelings of inferiority and experiencing temporary relief) the more deeply ingrained that memory association becomes. This is how unconscious habits are formed. Some of these habits may be healthy (i.e. buying fruit for snacks instead of junk food), and others (i.e. eating chocolate when you feel lonely), not so much!

Your challenge is to undo the unhealthy eating and lifestyle habits you've formed and begin developing and reinforcing healthier ones. For instance, I had an unconscious habit of reaching into my desk drawer for chewing gum whenever I sat down at my computer to write. NOT a good habit if one is trying to prevent belly bloat! My chewing gum habit started out as a desire to relieve the restless feeling I get whenever I'm forced to spend long hours writing while working on a post or a book manuscript. Each time I used the experience of chewing a piece of refreshing peppermint gum to ease that feeling, the behavior was reinforced by the pleasant sensations, taste, and uplifting feelings that were generated.

The first few times I engaged in the behavior it was a conscious decision – but, before long, that behavior became so "automatic" that I was going through a pack of gum a day and suffering from the negative consequences caused by the excess air I was swallowing and the artificial sweetener I was consuming. So, what started out being temporarily helpful, ended up creating increased negative physical, mental, and emotional consequences. I was physically bloated and felt "fat," disappointed in myself, and like all my healthy eating and exercising efforts were useless.

Let's dissect my chewing gum habit to further clarify this unconscious pairing process.

> Environmental Cue or Trigger: Sitting down at my computer to write

> Emotional Trigger: Feelings of restlessness or boredom

> Behavioral Response: Chewing gum

> Short Term Goal: Pleasure, distraction, emotional relief

> Short Term Consequences that Reward & Reinforce Behavior: Relief from negative emotions, pleasant taste, fresh breath, distraction of chewing and swallowing

> Conflicting Long Term Goal: Positive body image, nutritious eating, listening to and respecting my body

> Long Term Consequences: Chewing gum became an impulsive coping response to negative feelings and developed into an unconscious habit. Belly bloating that led to negative body image thoughts and feelings of defeat related to healthy eating and exercising (i.e. "I'm already bloated, what's the point of making a healthy dinner now?)

> End Result: Healthy lifestyle and eating intentions are sabotaged, self esteem and positive body image are undermined, and motivation level declines.

Does this process sound familiar? Does sitting down to watch a movie trigger an overwhelming desire to eat popcorn dripping with butter? Do you find yourself heading for the kitchen after seeing food advertisements on television? Has your morning commute become paired with stopping at Starbucks for a flavored coffee that's loaded with calories?

The difficulty with keeping long term goals related to healthy behavior arises when short term hedonistic goals are triggered, resulting in a goal conflict.

Without being consciously aware of your actions, your short term goal behavior is activated and inhibits behavior that leads to achieving your long term goals. In the above example, my short term goal of relieving the discomfort of my restless feelings overshadowed my long term goals of not feeling bloated or "fat," listening to my body, and maintaining a positive body image and nutritional eating.

WOW...nothing like one small, seemingly insignificant habit sabotaging a whole bunch of important long term goals!

You might be feeling a little pessimistic about your chances of ditching your disordered eating and achieving your long term healthy lifestyle goals right about now...but, just by being aware that goal conflicts exist and that you've been conditioned to respond to certain situations habitually is the first step to taking control over the process of forming habits.

Steps for Taking Control of Your Habits (Eating or Otherwise)

Step 1: Become aware of your environmental and emotional triggers that lead to goal conflicts.

Step 2: Set long term goals that are meaningful to you and that you're passionate about.

Step 3: Prime healthy behaviors by using goal-related words or environmental cues that trigger your motivation to engage in behavior that leads toward your long term goal attainment.

Step 4: Build structure into your daily routine that reinforces healthy eating and lifestyle habits.

- Use Post-It Notes to leave yourself reminders.
- Repeat affirmations or mantras daily.
- Create a vision or dream board that depicts your long term goal.
- Develop a plan for interrupting unhealthy or undesirable eating habits and replace these with long term goal-oriented behaviors and healthy NON-FOOD alternatives.
- Organize your life to make engaging in healthy behavior as easy as possible.

To deal with my chewing gum habit, I started to pay more attention to my automatic behaviors. Whenever I found myself reaching for my desk drawer, I interrupted the process by getting up and doing something physical (like squats or stretches) and telling myself that chewing gum is just a short term "fix" and that I really don't want to feel bloated and "fat." And, I made sure that my "moving" didn't include a trip to the kitchen!

What seemingly "innocent" habits do you have that are ultimately undermining your success in ditching disordered eating? (i.e. not voicing your opinion to keep the peace, drinking diet soda to give yourself a "pick me up," labeling foods as good vs. bad, stopping at Starbucks on your way to work or a fast food place whenever you've had a hectic day, etc.)

What short term vs. long term goal or motivation conflicts do you find yourself torn between? (i.e. short term emotional relief vs. long term weight and health goals, motivation to get fit for yourself vs. motivation to not change and expose yourself to ridicule, etc.)

How can you make your long term goals more meaningful? (i.e. make them more specific, add inspirational and progressive steps to help you achieve them, relate them more closely to your needs, make them more relevant to your desired vision of a happy and successful future, etc.)

Are there others in your life that are interfering with your long term goal attainment? (i.e. a significant other or friend who entices you to stray from your healthy intentions out of their fear that you'll "outgrow" or lose interest in them, etc.)

Part of raising your overall awareness is paying attention to how other people's behavior and attitudes affect your coping choices and lifestyle decisions. Take a closer look at your relationships. You might be surprised at what you discover. Just because a certain relationship "should" function in a supportive way doesn't mean that that's what's actually happening. For example, a mother who's adept at couching criticism in "helpful" advice undermines a child's self esteem and self confidence, increases their confusion about fitting in vs. belonging, and sends a very strong message that something is wrong with that child.

As you examine your relationships, consider the following questions:

- Are any of your relationships holding you back from realizing your goals? If so, which one(s).

- Which relationships are supportive and provide you with a strong sense of belonging?

- Who believes in you and sees your innate value?

- Who makes you feel bad after spending time with them?

Continue to explore your relationships, allowing yourself to be curious, open-minded and objective to what you discover. The influence the people you surround yourself with can make the difference between success and failure, between ditching your disordered eating and holding on tightly to a life preserver that is keeping you stuck in an unhealthy place, or worse, is destroying your physical, emotional, and mental health.

One of the most beneficial assertiveness skills you can master is setting appropriate and healthy personal boundaries that protect you physically, mentally, and emotionally. Depending on your responses to the relationship assessment questions, it might be time to set and/or reinforce healthier personal boundaries. Some relationships may not be worth the personal cost to you. Some may just need a healthy dose of assertive communication and an adjustment to expectations, while others may be in need of more authenticity on your part to deepen feelings of intimacy and connection. Still others may only require that you show them recognition and appreciation for how supportive and wonderful they already are!

Chapter 8

Physical Hunger vs. Emotional Hunger:
What are you REALLY Hungry For?

The sensation of physical hunger is satisfied with food. The emptiness of emotional hunger can only be satisfied with self care.

Disordered eating behavior can stem from your inability to accurately answer the question "What am I REALLY hungry for?" As previously mentioned, to determine if the hunger you're feeling is physically or emotionally driven you need to hone your interoceptive awareness. Interoception is a natural awareness of internal body states like hunger, pain, and organ movement and refers to the signaling and perception of these internal bodily sensations. It's the sensitivity to stimuli originating from within the body that includes the ability to identify both appetite signals and emotional cues.

Well-developed appetite awareness (AA) and emotional awareness (EA) have proven to be valuable skills to decrease disordered eating behavior and support a healthy relationship with food. The ability to correctly interpret hunger and satiety cues (AA), as well as, the ability to identify, acknowledge (EA), and express emotions are vital skills for recovering from disordered eating patterns and discovering that food is not the real problem behind your eating and weight related struggles. Research indicates that women who have lower levels of interoceptive awareness are more prone to eat (or not eat) for emotionally driven reasons rather than actual physiological hunger.

Are you misinterpreting your Hunger Cues?

Individuals who lack emotional awareness have difficulty identifying feelings, often misinterpreting their emotions as physical hunger and eating in response to the presence of intense emotions. Individuals who lack appetite awareness have difficulty recognizing their body's hunger and satiety cues that signal the presence of physiological hunger and when that has been satisfied. Interestingly, research indicates that having a higher degree of appetite awareness has more impact on eating behavior than does emotional awareness, although both are important skills for recovery.

Is your hunger driven for physiological reasons or emotional ones?

The first step in answering this question and raising your interoceptive awareness is to look at the difference between the cues your body gives you that stem from physical hunger and the cues it sends that spring from emotional hunger. The chart on the following page delineates the differences.

HUNGER CUES CHART

Physiological (physical) Cues	Emotional Cues
Feelings of hunger are gradual & progressive. (at least 2-3 hours after a meal & go from rumbling to growling, etc.)	Feelings of hunger are sudden & urgent. (no time frame, may have just eaten but feel "starved")
Hunger can be satisfied by any food. (you may have food preferences, but you're open to alternatives)	Hunger is for a specific type of food. (i.e. you're craving chocolate, pizza, or ice cream & no other food will do)
Hunger sensations originate from the stomach. (gnawing, rumbling, emptiness, even pain, dizziness & headaches may also occur)	Hunger cravings originate in the mind & mouth. (taste of specific food & thoughts center around that specific food)
Fullness is felt & acknowledged. The individual is able to stop eating once they feel satisfied.	Fullness is ignored. The individual continues to eat to numb emotions even when they are painfully stuffed. No amount of food can satisfy them.
*Results in feelings of Satisfaction and Contentment afterward.	***Results in feelings of Guilt, Shame, and Powerlessness afterward.**

The second step is paying attention to the intensity of your hunger level. The following scale can be used to rate your hunger level in your Food Relationship Journal (Ch. 9).

The Physical Hunger Scale

Individuals who are skillful at deciphering their body's interoceptive sensations (AA & EA) consistently stay in the middle of the Physical Hunger Scale and are much less likely to eat for emotional reasons. This scale ranges from Starving (1) to Satisfied (5-6) to Stuffed (10).

1. Starving, feeling weak & light headed from hunger.

2. Very uncomfortable, irritated & unable to concentrate, stomach is growling.

3. Uncomfortable, the hunger sensations have progressed to a gnawing feeling.

4. Slightly uncomfortable, starting to feeling rumbling sensations & think about food.

5. Comfortable, relatively satisfied but could eat more.

6. Perfectly comfortable, satisfied and content.

7. Full, with just a little discomfort.

8. Uncomfortably full, bloated.

9. Very uncomfortably full, clothes too tight & the need to relieve pressure on the stomach is present.

10. Stuffed, so full it hurts.

The ideal time to eat is BEFORE you get too hungry (in the 3-4 range). The ideal time to stop eating is BEFORE you become uncomfortably full (in the 5-6 range). Allowing yourself to get too hungry sets you up to overeat and eating to the point of physical discomfort can trigger feelings of guilt and shame.

Paying attention to your body's hunger and satiety cues empowers you to eat mindfully. Paying attention to your body's emotional cues empowers you to deal with your feelings and their true cause directly and proactively. Increasing your interoceptive awareness skills helps you to separate your emotions from food so you can deal with the underlying issues that drive your disordered eating, leading to a healthier relationship with food, yourself, and your body.

If your hunger is emotional, the answer is not in the fridge. The answer is figuring out what your unmet need is and then arming yourself with the necessary skills to deal with it.

After all, food is fuel, not therapy.

Chapter 9

Food Relationship Journal

"Your curiosity is your growth point. Always."

Danielle LaPorte

Some of you may shutter at the very thought of keeping a journal...writing is JUST NOT YOUR THING! Throw in having to track your food intake as a major part of the journal and your negative reaction to the whole idea intensifies to the point that you come up with every excuse in the book to procrastinate, forget, or downright refuse to engage in the process. But, if you'll indulge me a moment, I think I can persuade you on its merits. Let me start by defining what a Food Relationship Journal is. It may not be what you're thinking. And, it doesn't require great writing skills, a ton of time, or guilt!

Keeping a Food Relationship Journal is one of the most effective ways to determine the connection between how you're feeling and your food choices and behavior. It's NOT a food journal > it's a food *and* feelings journal. It's designed to help you discover the connection between your eating behavior and your emotions.

If you can discover the connection...you have the power to DISCONNECT! The purpose (and the power) of the journal is to raise your awareness of the buried issues that are driving your disordered eating and help you understand that food in and of itself is NOT the problem. Your weight is NOT the problem. Your body is NOT the problem. The problem goes much deeper and often has to do with your unmet needs.

But, because we live in a society that is focused on outward appearances, unrealistic beauty standards, and a misguided definition of success, it's hard not to confuse wanting to fit in with needing to belong. This desire to fit in at all costs pushes us to disconnect from our authentic selves and our bodies in an attempt to look, think, and act like the "beautiful people" held up as the gold standard of how everyone "should" be.

Your need for esteem (both self esteem and the esteem of others) can get entangled with this goal to fit in but also be recognized for your accomplishments. That's how losing "x" amount of pounds, *by whatever means necessary,* becomes a reasonable (in your mind) way to get these needs met. It's more concrete and easier to understand.

The problem with this line of thinking is that the solution is temporary and doesn't address the real cause of your unpleasant feelings. You've merely buried your more complicated concerns that require a complex set of skills to solve and a willingness to face your feelings beneath the less complicated issues of "being too fat, too heavy, too unattractive" and begun using disordered eating as a way to cope. Your relationship with food has become unhealthy and your food related choices symbolize these underlying issues instead of reflecting the mindset that food is a source of energy and pleasure.

What needs to be in a Food Relationship Journal?

You may be worried that documenting your eating behavior will lead you to become even more obsessed about food or ashamed about what you've been eating. But, remember, this is NOT an exercise in guilt, it's an *exploration* of the connection between eating behavior and feelings. Think of yourself as an investigative reporter whose goal is to gather unbiased information. Approach the journaling process with nonjudgmental curiosity. The information gathered is merely data that you can use to make healthier decisions.

The journal needs to include:

- Date
- Time
- What you ate
- What you were doing, thinking and feeling before you ate
- Hunger rating (Use the Physical Hunger Scale from the previous chapter.)

Gathering this information will increase your emotional awareness (EA). Over time you'll begin to notice patterns and start to see a few "regular" emotions that keep emerging as triggers to your disordered eating behavior. As this list of emotions solidifies, dig deeper to discover their root cause. Learning the root source allows you to identify skills you may be lacking and provides you with the opportunity to address the problem directly.

The data gathered in the journal can also be used to raise your appetite awareness (AA). Give yourself a hunger rating on a scale of 1-10, with "1" being famished, "10" being miserably stuffed, and "5" being neither hungry nor full, but neutral. If you rate yourself before and after you eat, you can track all kinds of useful information. For instance, you can determine if you're waiting too long to eat and that's actually causing you to overeat or if following a strict diet is creating feelings of deprivation that build until you end up binging on an entire bag of chips without even tasting them.

Tracking these two pieces of information, feelings and physiological hunger, helps you develop your interoceptive awareness, an essential empowerment skill to ditching your disordered eating as a coping strategy. Interoceptive awareness includes both emotional awareness and appetite awareness. Developing your interoceptive awareness skills helps you to start listening to your body again. You begin recognizing hunger and satiety cues, you being recognizing and acknowledging the range of emotions you feel, and you begin interpreting the messages your food choices are sending you.

After you've been documenting your interoceptive awareness long enough to see the emerging patterns and identify emotional triggers and deeper issues, you may want to start keeping track of alternative coping strategies that you try and how well they work. This adds the extra benefit of creating an outline for a proactive stress management plan that you can use to augment a healthy lifestyle and your overall life fitness. The information you gather in your Food Relationship Journal can also guide you in identifying other skill areas that you may need to become more proficient in (media literacy, assertiveness, emotional intelligence, self care).

In the beginning you may still find yourself coming up with a multitude of excuses to not keep the journal. You're too busy, you have too many other commitments, you have other things that seem more important to spend your time on, you "forget," your dog buried the journal...etc. This resistance is a perfectly normal response to the threatening activity of shedding light on your eating behavior. Don't waste time beating yourself up over it. Just remind yourself that the Food Relationship Journal is designed to function the exact opposite of what your disordered eating is designed to do.

The function of the food relationship journal is to bring your emotions and deeper issues into your conscious awareness while the function of your disordered eating is to keep them out.

Chapter 10

How Your Relationship With Your Body Affects Your Relationship With Food

"Your relationship with love is your relationship with the essence of who you are. It affects your relationship with your body, and your relationship with food. When you realize that you are a spirit and that this body is a temple, then you want to treat it well."

Marianne Williamson

The relationship you have with your body is encapsulated in your body image – how you think and feel about your body. If you have a positive and accurate body image, accepting and loving your body just as it is, you'll appreciate all the amazing things that it does for you. You'll see your body as your home, your ally, your protector – and, you'll treat it well.

If, however, your body image is negative and distorted, you're likely to punish it by stuffing it, starving it, neglecting it, over exercising or even surgically modifying it. Instead of feeling love and respect for your body, a negative body image promotes feelings of self-loathing and self-destructive actions. It leads to feelings of detachment from your body that cause you to de-value and stop listening to it. Your body has become the enemy and food has become a weapon you can use in your war against it.

The better you treat your body, in word and in deed, the better able it is to serve you and the better your relationship with it will become.

This connection between your relationship with food and your relationship with your body is targeted in the empowering actions brought about by mastering the life skills detailed in the previous chapter. Here's how that looks when the "rubber hits the road" and these life skills are put into action:

1. Reframing how you think about food helps you make nutritional choices that fuel your body according to it's energy needs, instead of feeding your emotional hunger.

2. Accepting and loving your body provides the motivation to improve your interoceptive awareness and start listening to it again. You begin to respect and identify physical hunger and satiety cues. And, you begin to become more aware of your emotions, seeing them as indicators of problems, but also indicators of when all is going well.

3. Increasing your emotional intelligence enhances your ability to correctly identify and feel all of your emotions, to learn from them instead of stuffing them or being overwhelmed by them. You understand that emotions aren't good or bad and they can't hurt you – only your actions in response to these emotions can. Your knowledge allows you to choose your response rather than act out in harmful ways or avoid dealing with negative feelings and using food to self-medicate.

4. Practicing self care shows your body that you're invested in taking good care of it, emotionally, mentally, and physically and, in return, it will serve you to the best of its ability.

5. Communicating assertively helps you deal with conflicts directly, voice your thoughts and emotions appropriately, and stand up for and protect yourself. You'll experience fewer food cravings, and, instead, seek healthy ways to get your needs met.

6. Becoming a media critic opens your eyes to advertising manipulation and to the subtle ways you're being sold the false idea that you aren't good enough the way you are. That to be worthy you must conform to cultural ideals of beauty, success, and prestige.

By mastering the aforementioned empowerment skills you'll become your own best friend and advocate, you'll joyfully define beauty and success in your own way, and you'll "see" and appreciate the beauty and uniqueness of others.

You'll embody love – for yourself and for others. Your inner beauty will define you, not your outward appearance, and the relationships you have with yourself, your body, and food will heal.

Heal Thy Self = Healthy Self

TIPS TO BUILD A BETTER BODY IMAGE

You can build a better body image, starting right now, today! The only thing you have to lose is your negative perceptions – you have the power to change how you experience your body and your life. Below are some simple ways you can begin to accept, love, and nurture your body.

Accepting your body:

- Embrace your body and show gratitude for all of the wonderful functions it performs – from breathing to protecting you to getting you from point "A" to point "B." Write your body a *"Gratitude Letter"* detailing everything great that it's capable of doing and apologizing for the ways in which you've abused it (poor or disordered eating, over or under exercising, risk-taking behavior, neglect, etc.). End your letter with a promise to treat it better – with kindness, love, nurturance, and appreciation.

- *Balanced Beauty Self-Assessment*: Look in the mirror, but this time, instead of focusing on your perceived flaws, intentionally focus your attention to appreciation of what you like about your body. Spend as much time on your body's good parts as its bad. See yourself with the "balance" that everyone else naturally already sees. Practice seeing yourself with new eyes, let the perspective of how loving others see you remind you of what it is you're looking for when you gaze in the mirror.

Loving your body:

- *Shut down the critical voice* in your head that tells you that your body isn't "right" or that you're weak or are a bad person because your body isn't the social or media "ideal." *Turn up the volume on the kinder, gentler voice* that speaks lovingly and admiringly to yourself.

- Become a critical viewer of social and media messages rather than your body and yourself.

- Wear clothes that are comfortable, show your style, and make you feel good about your body.

Nurturing your body:

- Do nice things for yourself, ones that let your body know you appreciate it. Eat healthy, get plenty of rest, enjoy a massage or spa day, engage in a regular fitness routine, etc.

- Celebrate & get comfortable with your body through movement and dance. Let go of bodily tension and negativity.

- Engage in a regular relaxation routine (deep breathing, progressive muscle relaxation, meditation, yoga, stretching, etc.).

- Develop and utilize a stress management plan that targets physical, mental, and emotional stress.

*Refer to How To "Rock" Your Body Image for more in-depth ways to address body image issues.

Above all, STOP WORRYING ABOUT WHAT OTHER PEOPLE THINK and begin freeing yourself from unrealistic and potentially unhealthy beauty standards – create your own vision of beautiful!

Making a shift in your perspective is a key component to transforming your life – to ditching disordered eating and developing a healthy relationship with food and your body. The next example shows just how powerful this kind of shift can be in "seeing" yourself differently and the many reasons you have to be grateful for your uniqueness, your inner strength, and all of the qualities that make you who you are.

Forensic Sketches: Perception is in the Eye of the Beholder

A forensic sketch artist is asked to make sketches of women according to the descriptions he is given. He doesn't see the women until after he is all finished, nor do they see him.

Each woman is sketched twice – once from her own description and once from the description given by another woman who had been told "get to know" her. The women did not know the purpose of the exercise, only that they should get friendly with the other woman.

The forensic artist led each woman to provide information to help him draw the sketches:

Tell me about your (her) hair.
Tell me about your (her) eyes.
And, your (her) nose?
What about your (her) cheekbones?
Tell me about your (her) chin.

Your (her) jaw?
What would be your (her) most prominent feature?

And so on until the sketches were complete. After all of the sketches were finished, the forensic artist brought each woman in to look at the two sketches he had done of them. The women were amazed at the differences between the two sketches.

The women made remarks about their sketches like: "She looks closed off and fatter and sadder (from the woman's own description) while the second sketch (from the other woman's description) looks more open, friendlier, happier and much thinner."

When asked what they had gotten from the exercise the responses echoed each other: They should be more grateful for their natural beauty. They emphasized that how we perceive ourselves impacts everything – the choice in friends we make, the jobs we apply for, how we treat ourselves, our children and others.

Takeaway: As women we spend a lot of time analyzing ourselves critically, looking for flaws and trying to fix the things that aren't quite right. Instead, we need to refocus our "lens" and spend more time looking for and appreciating the things we like about ourselves.

It's human nature to "see" what we're looking for. Why not see the beauty, wisdom and inherent worth in ourselves?

WE ARE MORE BEAUTIFUL THAN WE THINK!

SUMMARY:

Not only are you more beautiful than you think, you're more powerful. You have the ability to change your mindset about food. You have the ability to choose the thoughts that you fuel and the habits that you reinforce. If you look deep inside yourself, you'll find the courage, the strength, and the wisdom to do what's right for you. You can learn to love and accept all parts of yourself – to "see" yourself differently. You have the power within you to reset your relationship with food, yourself and your body. You're capable of developing the skills necessary to ditch your disordered eating and embrace the freedom and joy of a healthy life without it!

But, you don't have to do it alone. One of the most empowering things you can do for yourself is to reach out for support and guidance when you're struggling. Love yourself enough to lean on others when you need to. Have faith that in time, you'll be skilled enough to "swim" on your own.

Celebrate!

By reading this book you've already started transforming your life! What you know, you cannot unknow and this knowledge will inform your actions going forward, even if the changes seem small and insignificant at the time.

Additional Self Help Books by This Author

Stress Management 2.0 Series:

Mental Stress Management 2.0: 40 Tips For De-Cluttering Your "Inner Closet"

Book 1 of the Stress Management 2.0 series. Essential resource of 40 powerful tips to help you manage your stress in the moment and over the long term. Use them to clear your mind of harmful, self-defeating thoughts and beliefs and make room for creative thinking, positive thoughts and feelings, and new, empowering beliefs.

Emotional Stress Management 2.0: 40 Tips For Taming Your Turbulent Emotions

Book 2 of the Stress Management 2.0 series. Essential resource of 40 effective tips to tame chaotic emotions and reduce your emotional stress level. Use these targeted strategies to bring yourself back to a state of calm and restore your ability to respond to challenges and frustrations productively. These powerful techniques will also help you to de-clutter the emotional space in your "inner closet" and create room to savor and store positive and peaceful feelings.

Stress Management Blueprint 2.0: Design Your Own Stress Relief Plan

Book 3 of the Stress Management 2.0 series. Crucial resource that provides a blueprint for designing a stress relief plan that targets both chronic and acute stress, is well-balanced, and is tailored to fit your individual needs and preferences. Use it in combination with Book 1 and 2 of the Stress Management 2.0 series to build a powerful, effective stress management plan that is flexible and based on goals and techniques you've chosen for yourself.

The Fitness Goal Triad: How to Successfully Reach Your Fitness Goals

Guide to setting effective, realistic goals that target all three components of life fitness: body fitness, mind fitness, and emotional fitness. Learn how your thoughts and feelings impact your ability to reach your body fitness goals. Discover how to deal with your fluctuating motivation levels and bad attitude days. Included: progress monitoring tools and a sample goal plan.

How To "Rock" Your Body Image: Improve Body Image & Self Confidence

Guide to accepting and loving your body and yourself, recognizing and improving body image issues, dealing with "fat" days, and redefining beauty. Learn how to build your body confidence and self-esteem by becoming the best version of yourself.

Anorexia Athletica & Hypergymnasia: When Exercise Becomes an Obsession

Cutting edge resource for individuals, coaches, parents, and fitness professionals who work with athletes and committed exercisers and who want to be able to recognize and understand the symptoms and harmful effects of excessive training/exercise. Learn about risk factors, underlying personality traits, red flags of problem behaviors, and positive ways to intervene and promote a healthy sport or gym culture. Exercise Addiction Questionnaire included.

Journey To Self Empowerment: Increase Self Esteem & Self Confidence

The empowering ideas and suggestions in this book will help you take active control of your life, bolster your self esteem, and increase your self confidence. You'll learn how to stay empowered within relationships, set and enforce healthy boundaries, embrace being alone, change your mindset, and develop the inner strength you already have.

How To Get An "Emotional Divorce" & Speed Up Your Relationship Recovery

Essential guide to gaining the emotional detachment necessary to let go of a past relationship. Discover how to gain your emotional freedom by learning how to release toxic emotions, shift how you think about yourself and relationships, and take other vital recovery-based actions that will speed up your healing process.

Divorce Recovery: How To Clean Out Your "Inner Closet"

A critical guide to finding your way to a healthy Divorce Recovery that includes a happy and successful future. Find out how The 10 R's of Divorce Recovery can help you deal with the challenges you face. Re-discover yourself, clarify what you want in your life, and open yourself to an exciting, new chapter in your life.

All published titles are currently available on Amazon.com.

❖   Workshops and/or trainings available by author upon request.

Contact author at www.sagebrushcoaching.com or www.disorderedeatingguardian.com.

About the Author

Stephanie Eissinger is a Licensed Clinical Professional Counselor, Certified Professional Coach, Certified Embody Love Movement Facilitator, and Self Help book author who's dedicated her life to empowering individuals to recover from life's challenges to lead happier, healthier lives. She has both personal and professional experience dealing with disordered eating, excessive exercising, divorce/relationship recovery, grief, and stress management.

She has a small Coaching practice but is currently devoting most of her time to writing, speaking, and facilitating workshops in order to serve a greater number of people...no matter where they reside. Stephanie resides with her husband and has three grown children, two daughters and a stepson...all of whom are busy building successful lives of their own.

Made in the USA
Lexington, KY
19 June 2019